LOVE
LISTS
NOTES
& Me!

xxx

First published in the UK by Sleeping Lions Publishers

Illustration & Text Copyright © 2021 by Nikki Fuller

All rights reserved.

Sleeping Lions Publishers

LOVE LISTS NOTES & Me!

xxx

This is me!

↑...photo/doodle of me.

"Shine my light brightly…"

"Please have fun with this book. I have deliberately not put chapters in any particular order because I want you to dip in where you want, when you want...

...Write a few words, doodle,

pause for thought or build dreams.

Write wish lists,

to-do lists for anything & everything!

...We just love lists!

Pop notes in between the pages, articles you've cut out, postcards & photos.

If you need, stretch an elastic band around this book to keep your thoughts, dreams & wishes safe.

Use YOUR 'Love, Lists, Notes & ME' just for YOU & with a smile ...and a cup of tea & a chocolate biscuit.

With love your fellow lover of paper, lists & notes!"

"Don't outsource my own wellbeing..."

BETWEEN YOU & ME...

Especially after recent times, whether we like it or not life continually evolves; we cannot hold onto the status quo. We can be present in the moment but good and bad will always rotate and follow each other.

What we can do is find a way to ease ourselves back in gently, be aware of what's happening around us, work on new lists, new habits and tick them off.

Choose to react with our choice of emotion to an event and not allow the actual event to control or define us.

Be flexible with our intensions and dreams, move calmly with the ever changing flow.

It's okay not to over complicate things and overwhelm yourself; Choosing a simpler life.

> Recognise and know what looks
> and **feels enough for you.**

Trust your desires and respect and honour your own individual pace. Know there is a difference between settling, not being ambitious or playing it safe to recognizing **at this moment** you're already where you should be and where you need to be.

Let's dip in!...

CONTENTS...

✏️ BEING ME

✒️ CHOICES AND COURAGE

✏️ WISE WORDS & LESSONS

✒️ HEAD, HEART & KINDNESS

✏️ POSITIVE 'PAWS' FOR THOUGHTS

✒️ THOUGHTFUL DAYS Serve with tea & biscuits

✏️ LIGHTEN UP & unburden myself

✒️ TAP INTO MY CREATIVE SIDE

✏️ THE CHILD IN ME

✒️ 'FRIENDSHIPS'

✏️ PLANS, ADVENTURES & DREAMS

✏️ FILLS MY SOUL

✏️ For the LOVE of LISTS

✒️ THANK YOU...

BEING ME...

 BEING ME

Dear Me,

How am I?... What makes me, me? ...
(Write a letter to myself)

I ....
Am a Freedom Hunter
& choose happiness.
✐Signed:..................................
Date:......./......./......

 BEING ME

..."Be true & honest with myself."

 BEING ME

..."I'm really happy to be me."

🖉 BEING ME

..."If my mind can conceive it &
my heart can believe it,
I can achieve it."

 BEING ME

..."Breath out everything that is no longer kind to me."

 BEING ME

..."Nurture my self compassion:
Treat myself kindly,
Imperfection is okay,
I am not alone,
& keep perspective...
Choose a 'mellow drama'
over a melodrama."

 BEING ME

..."Choose MY OWN path."

 BEING ME

..."Don't put pressure on myself, it won't help me or those around me."

🖉 BEING ME

..."Write my own story, be the director of my own film memoir of **MY LIFE**...
Edit it, rewrite it, change directions,
...The power is mine!"

 BEING ME

..."Believe in myself and
my instincts...
It's **MY TRUE NORTH.**"

 BEING ME

..."Always be **true to myself**,
Some may not like it,
BUT better that
Than a life in hiding."

BEING ME

..."It's not ME against the WORLD
BUT
ME against **ME**."

 BEING ME

..."WHAT KIND OF PERSON WOULD I LIKE TO BECOME?"

 BEING ME

..."Being true to myself...
WILL SET ME **FREE!**"

✏️ BEING ME

..."Whether it's a small step or a leap, they all matter and keep me **moving forward.**"

 BEING ME

..."My job is to simply find a way to be happy with **ME**."

 BEING ME

..."TODAY... I will only do things that mean the most to me and to the ones I love."

BEING ME

..."I am enough,
I know enough,
I have enough..
So— **I CAN DO THIS!**"

 BEING ME

..."If I am doing my BEST-
I am doing ENOUGH."

BEING ME

Dear Self,
I hear you,
I care for you.
I will be kind to myself:
- ...make myself a tea
- ...buy myself some flowers
- ...do something that makes me happy

Signed:..................................
Date:......./......./......

CHOICES
& COURAGE...

🖊 CHOICES AND COURAGE

..."Take time...
...STOP, BREATH, REFLECT."

CHOICES AND COURAGE

..."Try being empathetic:
Not just to my dear friends and
family but to **MYSELF** too."

CHOICES AND COURAGE

..."Embrace the rhythm of my life:
IN HALE
STOP
BE STILL
EXHALE
BE STILL."

CHOICES AND COURAGE

..."Use my HEAD and my HEART,
And decide what is right for ME."

🖋 CHOICES AND COURAGE

..."Let my quiet, kind inner voice;
ENCOURAGE ME,
MOTIVATE ME,
BELIEVE IN MYSELF.
Focus on that quiet voice over the
loud voice that pulls me down."

CHOICES AND COURAGE

..."**Choose to escape** and step in to MY safe and happy place.... Fill my senses with music, smells and memories that nurture **ME**."

CHOICES AND COURAGE

..."BRAVERY &
being COURAGIOUS
Brings me **FREEDOM**."

CHOICES AND COURAGE

..."Have the **courage** to look after myself before I can look after others."

CHOICES AND COURAGE

..."Have the COURAGE to do
what **I WANT**
&
Not what is EXPECTED."

CHOICES AND COURAGE

..."Everything is a CHOICE,
what will I CHOOSE?"

CHOICES AND COURAGE

..."Sometimes making a change
can feel MESSY.
But when things are MESSY,
change is happening.
-Which means
PROGRESS & OPPORTUNITY.
Just by knowing this
it can be such a relief.
So when I am feeling
OUT OF CONTROL...
Just LET GO.
It's how it's supposed to be."

CHOICES AND COURAGE

..."Give myself **PERMISSION**...
...TO BE HAPPY,
...TO DO WHAT I LOVE,
...TO FOLLOW MY DREAMS."

CHOICES AND COURAGE

..."If I am feeling like not much is making sense, **change is happening** & I am about to get closer to being my true self."

CHOICES AND COURAGE

..."LOSING CONTROL =
POSSIBILITIES
OPPORTUNITIES
MIRACLES!"

CHOICES AND COURAGE

..."I don't need to TRAVEL to FREE MYSELF. It's available **NOW** with the **CHOICES** I make everyday."

CHOICES AND COURAGE

..."Have the COURAGE to make
those difficult decisions.
The more difficult-
the **bigger the rewards.**"

✎ CHOICES AND COURAGE

..."My **CHOICES** have
CONSEQUENCES
& have the **POWER**
to take me in ANY direction."

CHOICES AND COURAGE

..."FEELING FREE...
Is MINE
For the MAKING,
TAKING,
ANY TIME,
AT ANY AGE...
It's a CHOICE."

CHOICES AND COURAGE

..."There are only ever
3 OPTIONS:
LIVE with it,
IMPROVE it,
CHANGE it."

CHOICES AND COURAGE

..."Pour COURAGE over my life &
see myself GROW."

CHOICES AND COURAGE

..."CHOOSE my emotions
WISELY:
When something or an
event happens:
STOP and THINK...
How am I going to
CHOOSE to react ?
I can't change events but I do
have the power to choose how I
feel and express myself.
...And if life does deal me a
terrible card— I'll cut myself
some slack and be kind to myself."

CHOICES AND COURAGE

..."Sometimes I just have to STOP
& **LOOK UP**, otherwise I
might miss a CROSSROAD."

CHOICES AND COURAGE

..."HOW DO I WANT TO FEEL?
Find MYSELF in the CHOICES that
I make every day."

✒ CHOICES AND COURAGE

..."I AM responsible FOR MY CHOICES—no one else."

WISE WORDS & LESSONS...

It's ok to rewrite your Life...

🖉 WISE WORDS & LESSONS

..."What if I fail?
BUT
What if I succeed!"

...STOP, BREATH, REFLECT."

WISE WORDS & LESSONS

..."None of us know what the
future holds for us -
But ...**what am I okay with?**"

✏️ WISE WORDS & LESSONS

'WORRY'
...Doesn't solve problems.
...Doesn't achieve anything.
...Won't make anything go away.
STOP THAT
MINDLESS CHATTER."

✏️ WISE WORDS & LESSONS

"CLEAR THE MIND AND
CHOOSE TO TRAVEL LIGHTER."

✏️ WISE WORDS & LESSONS

If I REALLY can't solve a
REAL problem that matters.
Ask myself...
"How can I care for myself
through this?"
...It's time to be kinder
and calmer on myself.

✏️ WISE WORDS & LESSONS

Regularly ask myself...
FROM 1-10...
"How am I feeling?"
BE HONEST AND AWARE OF
MY MIND & BODY.
If it's a low number,
don't ignore it.
ACKNOWLEDGE IT.
Then be kind to myself or
make changes NOW.

✏️ WISE WORDS & LESSONS

"HOW DO I WANT TO FEEL?"

✏️ WISE WORDS & LESSONS

..."MY LIFE IS HAPPENING
RIGHT HERE!
RIGHT NOW!"

WISE WORDS & LESSONS

..."To make **CHANGE** first find something **wrong in my life** ...And **ADMIT** to it."

WISE WORDS & LESSONS

..."Be the MASTER of my
OWN TIME...
Fitting work around LIFE
And not
LIFE around work."

✏️ WISE WORDS & LESSONS

..."What **could I do differently?**
If I have been hurt or exposed to
changes or the unexpected."

WISE WORDS & LESSONS

..."What wise words would a friend
tell me, that I find difficult
to tell myself?"

HEAD, HEART & KINDNESS...

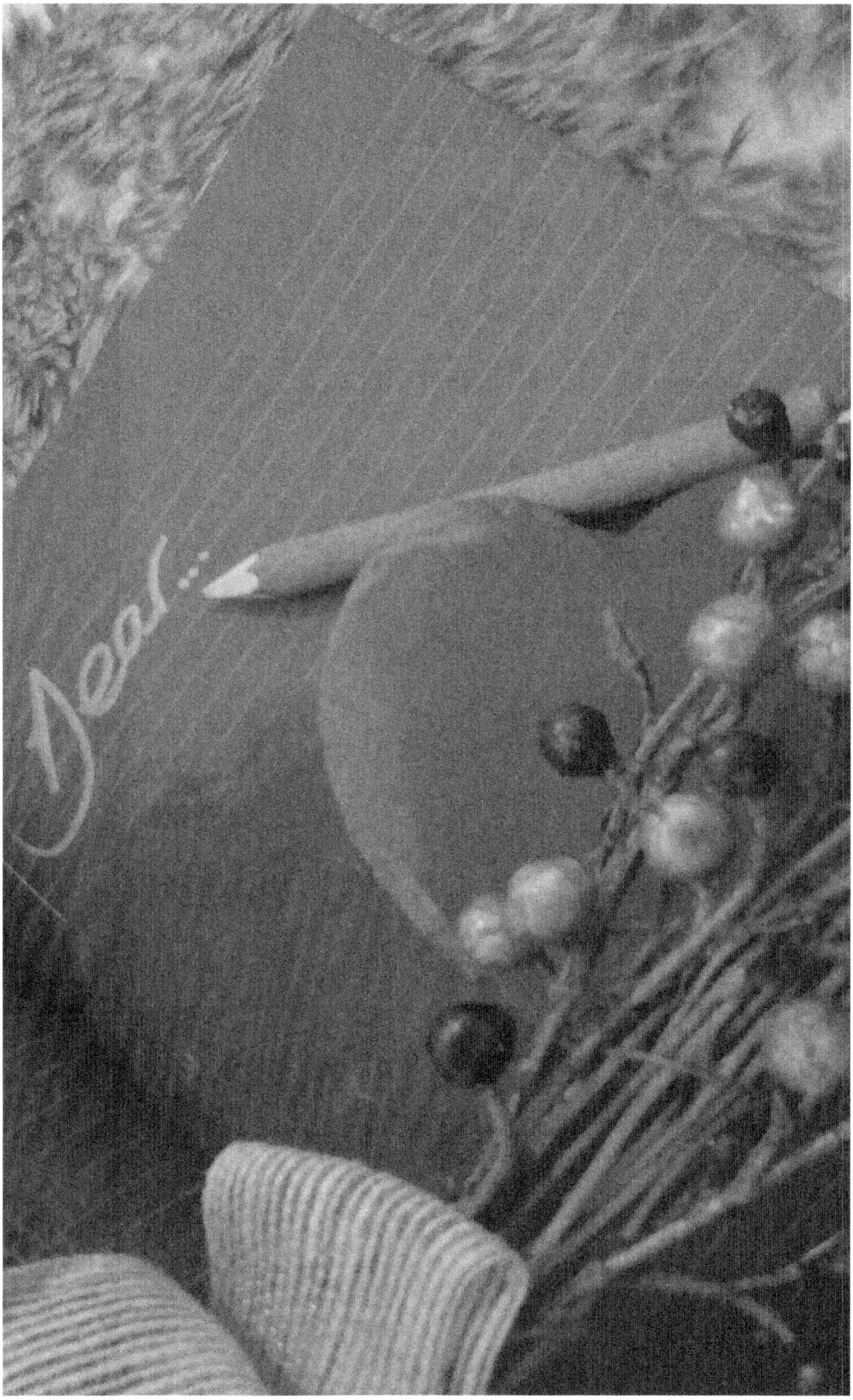
Dear...

HEAD, HEART & KINDNESS

..."HAPPINESS is what happens when you forget about trying to be happy."

✎ HEAD, HEART & KINDNESS

..."JUST LET GO!"

HEAD, HEART & KINDNESS

..."If I did my best and
I meant well...
Then that's **all I can do**."

HEAD, HEART & KINDNESS

..."I don't need to have all the ANSWERS...
...as long as I keep asking the **right QUESTIONS.**"

..."Stop looking over my shoulder, keep looking ahead otherwise I might miss an **opportunity**."

...*"Consider...*
That **everything** that I have
done up until now, was to prepare
me for this moment, this time.
Even the things that didn't
work out as I planned."

HEAD, HEART & KINDNESS

..."What if this is happening **FOR ME** and NOT TO ME? What if this leads to a better world for me?"

HEAD, HEART & KINDNESS

FREE MYSELF FROM THE
EXPECTATIONS OF OTHERS...

HEAD, HEART & KINDNESS

...TRYING TO CONTROL
EVERYTHING IS EXHAUSTING!
"Don't even try.
If I have a tendency to do this...
I HAVE TO STOP!
I can't control how others think,
what they do and the future.
BUT I can control:
How I react,
How I respond,
My choices
...And how I feel.

HEAD, HEART & KINDNESS

..."If I can talk myself
OUT of something-
I can talk myself
IN to something."

🖊 HEAD, HEART & KINDNESS

..."I SHOULD STOP TELLING MYSELF THE SAME OLD STORY & EXPECTING A DIFFERENT ENDING... **WRITE ONE THAT I LIKE."**

✒ HEAD, HEART & KINDNESS

..."With little steps I can still
make a good distance."

HEAD, HEART & KINDNESS

..."Letting go of being in CONTROL...
Doesn't mean I am not **POWERFUL**."

✐ HEAD, HEART & KINDNESS

..."I can give myself the GIFT
of **FORGIVENESS.**"

POSITIVE 'PAWS' FOR THOUGHTS...

PAUSE FOR THOUGHT

✏️ POSITIVE 'PAWS' FOR THOUGHTS

..."There's nothing much better than the softness of a puppy or kitten's ear."

POSITIVE 'PAWS' FOR THOUGHTS

…"BE THE LIGHT…
I am alive!
I am here—we are here."

✏️ POSITIVE 'PAWS' FOR THOUGHTS

..."I AM COURAGEOUS
I AM COURAGEOUS
I AM COURAGEOUS."

🖉 POSITIVE PAWS' FOR THOUGHTS

..."Who says my teddy bear isn't my best friend; loyal, always there and knows all my secrets."

✏️ POSITIVE PAWS FOR THOUGHTS

..."Live consciously...
Experience **LIVING**
not just
LIFE."

🖉 POSITIVE 'PAWS' FOR THOUGHTS

..."I am **STRONGER**
than I think
AND
More **COURAGEOUS** than I know."

POSITIVE PAWS FOR THOUGHTS

..."SURRENDER to the MOMENT
&
Conserve my power."

🖉 POSITIVE 'PAWS' FOR THOUGHTS

..."Please 'Bear' with me today—
I'm feeling a little anxious & fragile,
THANK YOU.."

POSITIVE 'PAWS' FOR THOUGHTS

Today I will not surround myself with people who:
WILL CRUSH MY DREAMS,
DISAPPROVE OF ME & MY WAYS.

POSITIVE PAWS FOR THOUGHTS

..."BEGIN WITH TODAY!"

POSITIVE 'PAWS' FOR THOUGHTS

..."I'll take the time to PAUSE
when I have a friend
who has PAWS!"

✏️ POSITIVE PAWS FOR THOUGHTS

To do...
OVER COMMITMENT ☒
SELF COMPARISON ☒
NEGATIVE SELF TALK ☒
CONTENTMENT ☑

THOUGHTFUL DAYS...

Best served with Tea & Biscuits...

MY THOUGHTS

✎ THOUGHTFUL DAYS...Best served with Tea & Biscuits

LIVE CONSCIOUSLY:
Spend the day how I would like,
Live to my values.
Choose what to eat,
Where to travel,
Who to spend time with,
How to relax.
SIMPLY BE AWARE
OF **HOW I FEEL**...

✐ THOUGHTFUL DAYS...Best served with Tea & Biscuits

..."Be THANKFUL & Be KIND."

THOUGHTFUL DAYS...Best served with Tea & Biscuits

"Sometimes just STOP.
Take time to THINK & LISTEN,
Become AWARE of the **PRESENT**."

✒ THOUGHTFUL DAYS...Best served with Tea & Biscuits

"Count my blessings EVERY day...
Start my day by thinking of
3 different things every morning."

THOUGHTFUL DAYS...Best served with Tea & Biscuits

"Today I will not take for granted,
what **means the most.**"

✏️ THOUGHTFUL DAYS...Best served with Tea & Biscuits

"How am I going to spend today?
...with GRATITUDE
& being FULLY AWARE"
And....

THOUGHTFUL DAYS...Best served with Tea & Biscuits

"It always seems IMPOSSIBLE
Until it is DONE."

✒ THOUGHTFUL DAYS...Best served with Tea & Biscuits

"Sometimes I need to know when to **REST** rather than give up."

LIGHTEN UP &
Unburden
myself...

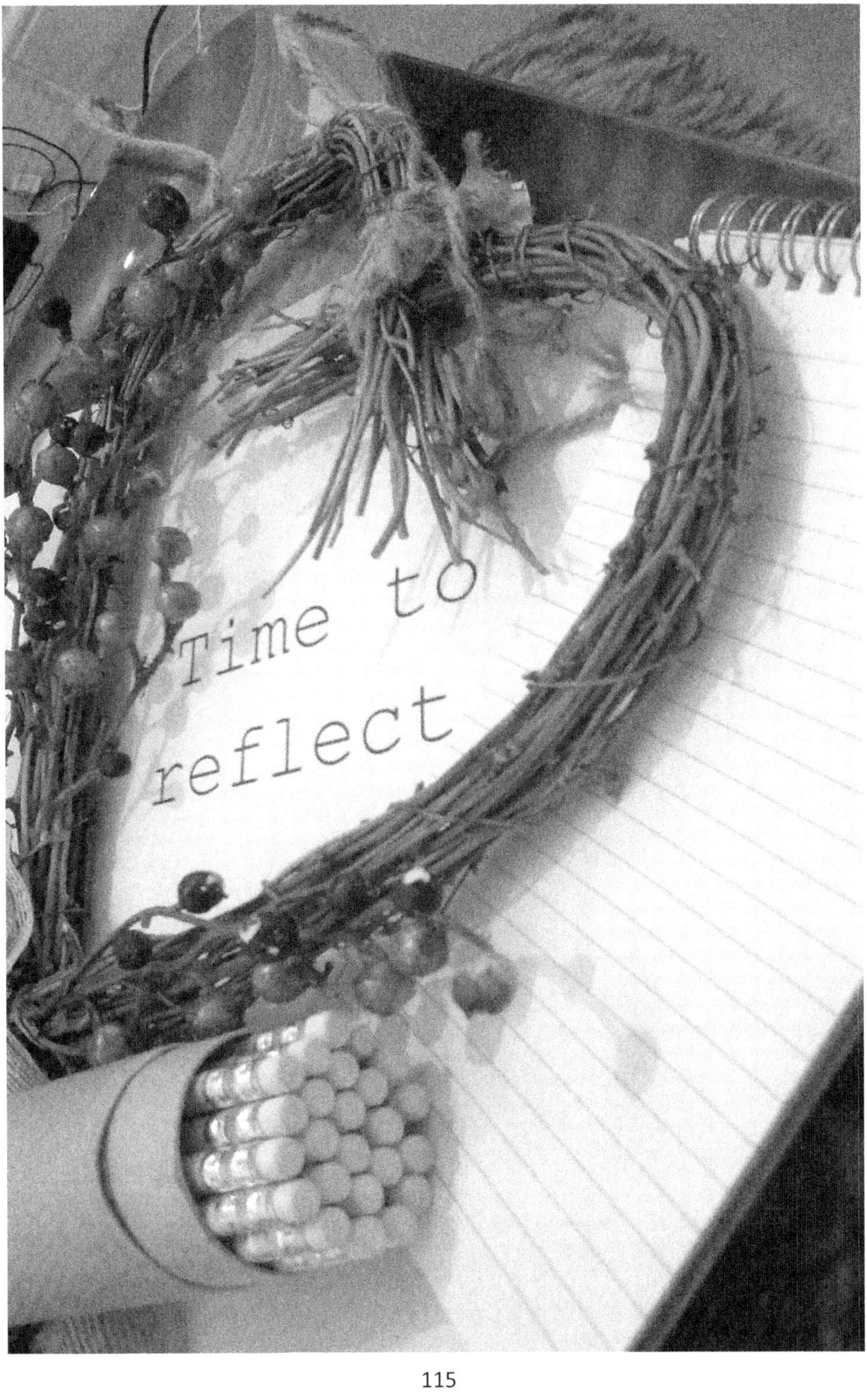
Time to
reflect

🖉 LIGHTEN UP & Unburden myself

..."FORGIVE MYSELF:
...For not doing things I planned
...For making mistakes
...For not being perfect
JUST DO MY BEST;
WATCH
LISTEN
LEARN
GROW
SMILE."

✏️ LIGHTEN UP & Unburden myself

..."It's OK to make mistakes
& forget to do things.
Just be **KIND & GENTLE** and
FORGIVE myself."

🖉 LIGHTEN UP & Unburden myself

..."**De-clutter** my home and my mind.
Ask myself:
Does it make me happy?
Do I need it?
IF NOT—Then **CLEAR IT OUT!**"

🖉 LIGHTEN UP & Unburden myself

..."Don't forget...
I have to FAIL to SUCCEED,
So give myself
PERMISSION to fail."

✏️ LIGHTEN UP & Unburden myself

..."Relinquish & Release!...
ANY constraints that I may have unconsciously placed on myself that are restricting me or stopping me from doing what makes me happy."

✏️ LIGHTEN UP & Unburden myself

..."Be **conscious** of these weights around me and where I can reduce them... **PRESSURES, RULES, GUILT, OBLIGATIONS.**"

✏️ LIGHTEN UP & Unburden myself

..."Nobody is perfect
AND
Nor do I have to be."

✏️ LIGHTEN UP & Unburden myself

..."My FAILURES are my
BEST LESSONS."

✏️ LIGHTEN UP & Unburden myself

..."**TEARS** can heal my pain.
TEARS will give me STRENGTH
and not weakness."

✏️ LIGHTEN UP & Unburden myself

..."FREE
MYSELF
from MYSELF."

✏️ LIGHTEN UP & Unburden myself

..."Learn to recognise
when I feel
TRAPPED in my
OWN EXPECTATIONS of myself and
Others EXPECTATIONS of ME."

✏️ LIGHTEN UP & Unburden myself

MY LIST OF THINGS
I DON'T LIKE OR I DON'T NEED:
sort into 4 groups with stickers...

RECYCLE = ☺

SELL £££ = £

GIVE IT AWAY = ⇨

RUBBISH = 🗑

✏️ LIGHTEN UP & Unburden myself

..."LIGHTEN MY LIFE!
De-clutter PHYSICAL ITEMS AND
NEGATIVE THOUGHTS
To make room for...
MY DREAMS & MY CHOICES."

✏️ LIGHTEN UP & Unburden myself

..."I AM **NOT RESPONSIBLE** FOR EVERYTHING & EVERYONE'S CHOICES."

TAP INTO MY
CREATIVE
SIDE...

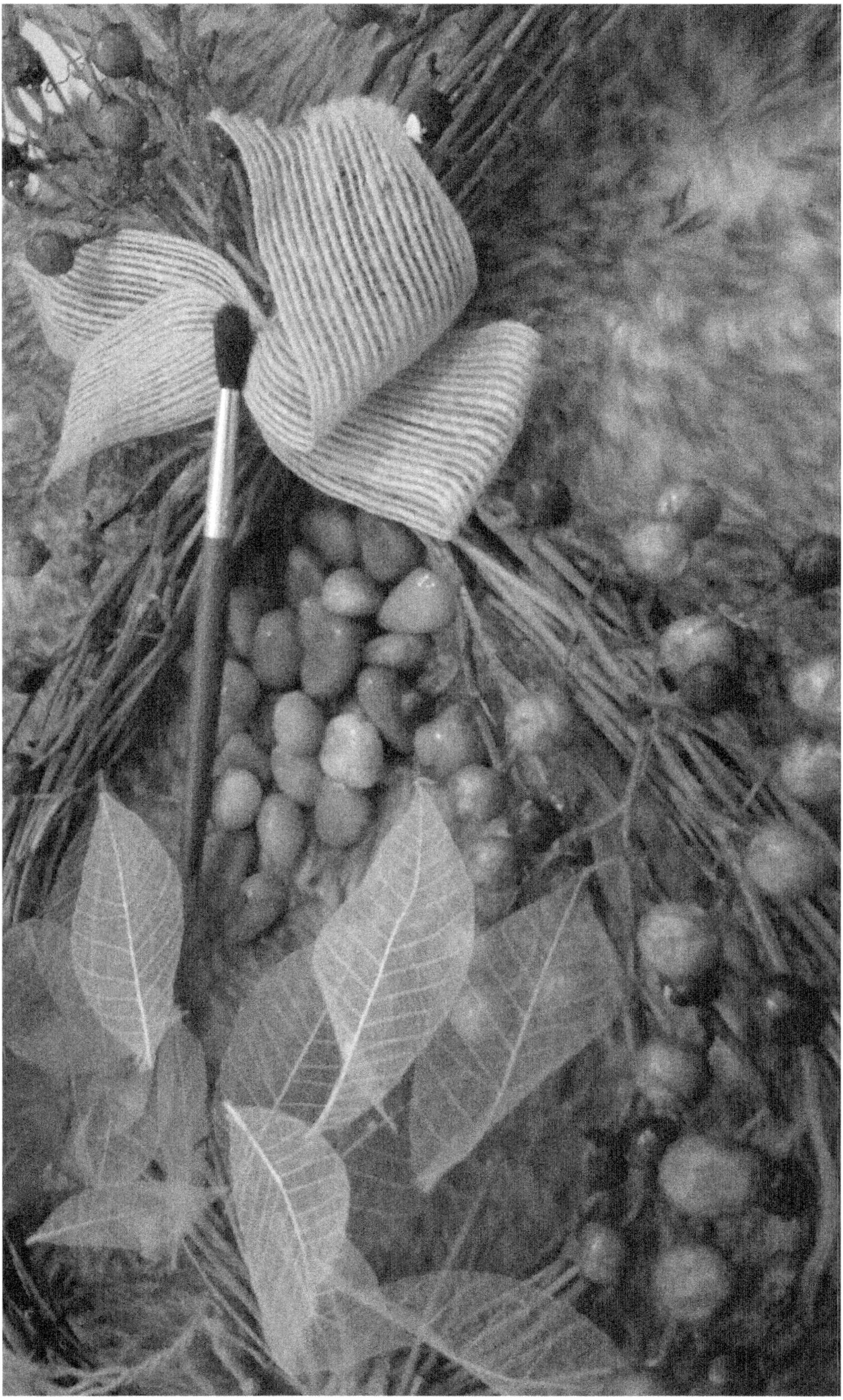

TAP INTO MY CREATIVE SIDE

"MY OBSERVATION GAME...
Pick something: E.g.. a model of a car,
a bike or a dog or even just a colour
AND...
...see how many I see in a day."

TAP INTO MY CREATIVE SIDE

"Exercise doesn't have to be **serious**...
I CAN...Dance in the kitchen,
Salsa when I brush my teeth or
wait for the kettle to boil,
Spell out my name with my hips!...
...To my favourite music."

TAP INTO MY CREATIVE SIDE

"**Seasons** help me to see natural beauty and they keep me moving forward—Remember to pick a few things through the seasons & decorate my home.
BRING THE OUTSIDE IN."

TAP INTO MY CREATIVE SIDE

"Hello my Creative self...
INSPIRE & EMPOWER ME!"

✒ TAP INTO MY CREATIVE SIDE

..."**CREATIVITY** is my **IMAGINATION** at **WORK**.
PAUSE, IMAGINE, CREATE...
...WRITE something
...MAKE something
...BUILD something
ANYTHING!... Just CREATE."

✒ TAP INTO MY CREATIVE SIDE

..."DEFEND my PERSONAL time,
Find what I love to do...
AND **DEFEND THIS** time."

✒ TAP INTO MY CREATIVE SIDE

"FEELING UNCREATIVE?...
Take the time to do something
that **inspires ME**:
READ A BOOK
WATCH A FILM
GO FOR A WALK
TALK TO A FRIEND
Imagine I have a watering can
that I need to fill with
creativity & inspiration...
Then pour where I need it;
...OVER MY LIFE &
WATCH MYSELF GROW."

TAP INTO MY CREATIVE SIDE

"Work on MY creativity
wherever & whenever
I choose that **inspires ME**."

✏️ TAP INTO MY CREATIVE SIDE

"Feed MY creative side
& express myself...
WRITE A LETTER
WRITE A POEM OR A SONG
MAKE NOTES FOR A BOOK
START A PROJECT... (with a new folder/notepad & pens!)
DRAW A PICTURE
SIMPLY DOODLE
MAKE SOMETHING
LEARN A NEW SKILL."

✒ TAP INTO MY CREATIVE SIDE

"USE NATURE TO INSPIRE ME...
Take the time,
to look,
listen and feel."

THE CHILD IN ME...

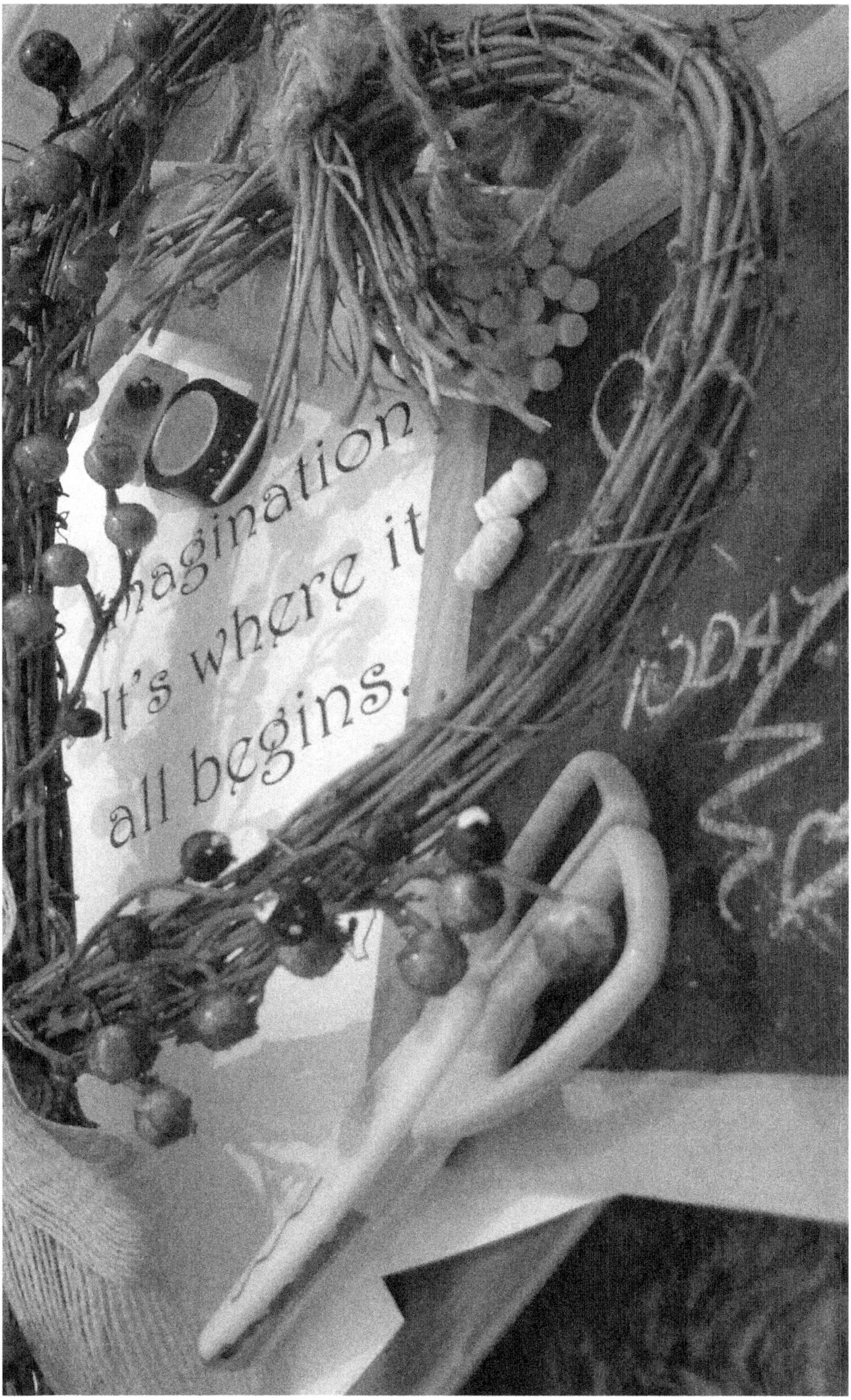
It's where it
all begins.

✏️ THE CHILD IN ME

..."Be more CURIOUS
Have FUN
Do something RANDOM
just because **I can**."

🖉 THE CHILD IN ME

REMEMBER...what made
me SMILE?...maybe:
...STRAWBERRY Milk Shakes
...LICKING THE CHOCOLATE
off a biscuit
...Making up a DANCE routine
...Walking down a path without
stepping on the CRACKS!
Have a little think & write a list. ☺

✏️ THE CHILD IN ME

..."Take time to **DAYDREAM,**
Daydreaming is where it all begins..
INSPIRATION & CREATIVITY."

✏️ THE CHILD IN ME

..."Find the CHILD within ME:
PLAY MORE
EXPLORE MORE
BE MORE CURIOUS."

✏️ THE CHILD IN ME

..."Today...I will lie in bed that little bit longer."

🖉 THE CHILD IN ME

..."BREATHE deeply through my nose
& inflate my **STOMACH,**
BREATHE out through my mouth &
deflate my stomach."

✏️ THE CHILD IN ME

"Move MY body more!"
...Stand on my tip toes,
...Suddenly run as fast as I can!
...Gallop rather than walk
...Wave my arms madly! & try not...
...TO SMILE.

THE CHILD IN ME

..."Pull a FUNNY FACE when I'm on
the phone to someone who is
annoying me &
feel myself **lighten up.**"

THE CHILD IN ME

..."Have a good GIGGLE."

..."LAUGH LOUDLY!"

✏️ THE CHILD IN ME

MY favourite...
COLOUR is:............................
ANIMAL is:............................
NUMBER is:...........................
WORD is:................................

✏️ THE CHILD IN ME

..."Never stop looking for what is not there...Free my **IMAGINATION** (...And find that Fairy Garden!)."

✏️ THE CHILD IN ME

..."Fill my MIND & HEART
with LOVE."

THE CHILD IN ME

..."Take a moment to think about MY favourite songs, TV shows & films **when I was younger**... Do I still like them?"

THE CHILD IN ME

..."When I was younger,
what did **I hope to be**?
Am I on the right path?"

FRIENDSHIPS...

Hi,
I thought I would write you a letter,
How are you?...

FRIENDSHIPS

..."There's nothing quite like a good catch up over a hot drink and a chocolate biscuit or a slice of cake."

FRIENDSHIPS

..."I shall never take YOU for
GRANTED...
Nor will I my COSY SLIPPERS,
The last square of CHOCOLATE.
The cream on my HOT CHOCOLATE
AND the
The first DAFFODILS of Spring."

FRIENDSHIPS

..."I LOVE YOU so much, I would share my last gingerbread biscuit with you at tea time."

FRIENDSHIPS

..."DAYDREAMING & BOREDOM
are my new 2 BEST FRIENDS...
It's where I can be
creative & make changes."

FRIENDSHIPS

..."WORDS UNITE...
They help us to help each other."

FRIENDSHIPS

..."But some day's it's OK to
NOT want to talk."

FRIENDSHIPS

..."**Surround myself** with people that inspire ME & energize ME"

FRIENDSHIPS

..."I like **PEOPLE** when they support, encourage, comfort & reassure me."

PLANS, ADVENTURES & DREAMS...

✏️ PLANS, ADVENTURES & DREAMS

..."PERSISTENCE is the KEY that will open more doors for me."

✏️ PLANS, ADVENTURES & DREAMS

..."Plant ONE seed at a time
What's **IMPORTANT**
not URGENT."

PLANS, ADVENTURES & DREAMS

..."HURRYING is like wind to a flame with my PRODUCTIVITY...
...They just don't go together."

🖉 PLANS, ADVENTURES & DREAMS

..."Worrying about not having **enough hours in the day** or simply a sense of
NOT ENOUGH TIME...
Will only:
INCREASE my STRESS,
My ANXIETY
And OVER WHELM me."

✏️ PLANS, ADVENTURES & DREAMS

..."SUCCESS is a PROCESS."

✏️ PLANS, ADVENTURES & DREAMS

..."THINGS that MATTER MOST,
Must never be at the **mercy** of
things that matter LEAST."

PLANS, ADVENTURES & DREAMS

..."**LIFE** is not about having all the GOOD CARDS dealt to me BUT... with the cards that I have been dealt, **knowing & learning how to** PLAY them well..."

✏️ PLANS, ADVENTURES & DREAMS

..."PAUSE, REFLECT & BREATHE
...Clear the FOG,
So I can SEE where
I need to GO."

✏️ *PLANS, ADVENTURES & DREAMS*

..."Give myself **PERMISSION** to do
what I LOVE,
And by doing so,
it becomes contagious...
Others will do the same...
If I am happy, they're happy &
If THEY'RE happy, I am happy."

PLANS, ADVENTURES & DREAMS

MY JAR OF LIFE...
How am I filling it today?

BIG STONES = My dreams, what I enjoy, my happiness, Goals & what's important to ME.
SHINGLE = Administration & Cleaning.
SAND = Trivial bits & pieces.

...If I fill my jar with sand and shingle <u>first</u>, I won't be able to put in my BIG STONES!
...So I must place my BIG STONES in FIRST then sprinkle around them the shingle and sand.

✏️ PLANS, ADVENTURES & DREAMS

MAKE MY DREAMS HAPPEN!

✏️ PLANS, ADVENTURES & DREAMS

..."Come ALIVE!
And find myself an **ADVENTURE.**"

PLANS, ADVENTURES & DREAMS

..."Doing things **I ENJOY**;
It's not selfish **BUT SELFCARE**."

PLANS, ADVENTURES & DREAMS

..."Living MY DREAMS is where MY
LIFE STARTS
Not ends..."

FILLS MY
SOUL...

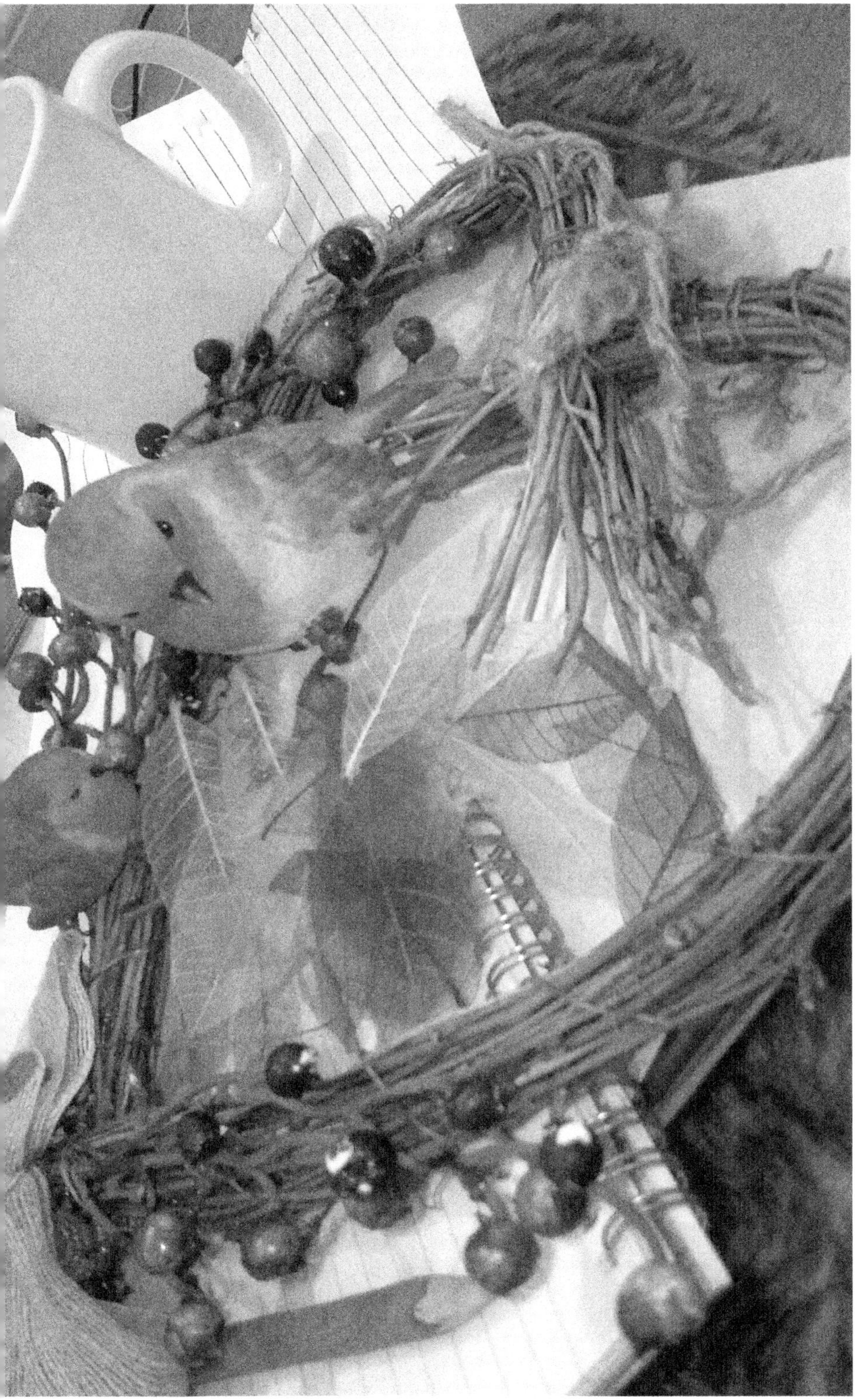

...FILLS MY SOUL

..."FLOWERS make my soul SMILE."

✒ ...FILLS MY SOUL

LISTEN TO...
THE WIND
THE BIRDS
MY OWN BREATH
...And find my **INNER CALMNESS.**

...FILLS MY SOUL

..."**HAPPINESS** is like a string of fairy lights, small glimpses of light, little moments one after the other...
...just a **string of MOMENTS strung together.**
Don't worry about the bigger picture & just enjoy each MOMENT;
BIG or SMALL."

...FILLS MY SOUL

..."Being OUTSIDE can give ME
PERSPECTIVE.
If it's all getting too much—
Remember to STEP outside."

✎ ...FILLS MY SOUL

..."NATURE does not know how to HURRY...
SHARE the JOURNEY."

✎ ...FILLS MY SOUL

..."Feeling the sand between my toes,
Blades of grass under my feet,
The fragrance of a flower,
Nature letting me know it's there...
...Fills my SOUL."

...FILLS MY SOUL

..."The TRUTH is in our HEARTS CHALLENGED by our HEADS & ANCHORED by our SOUL."

...FILLS MY SOUL

..."Being around those I LOVE, nurtures me."

For the LOVE
of Lists...

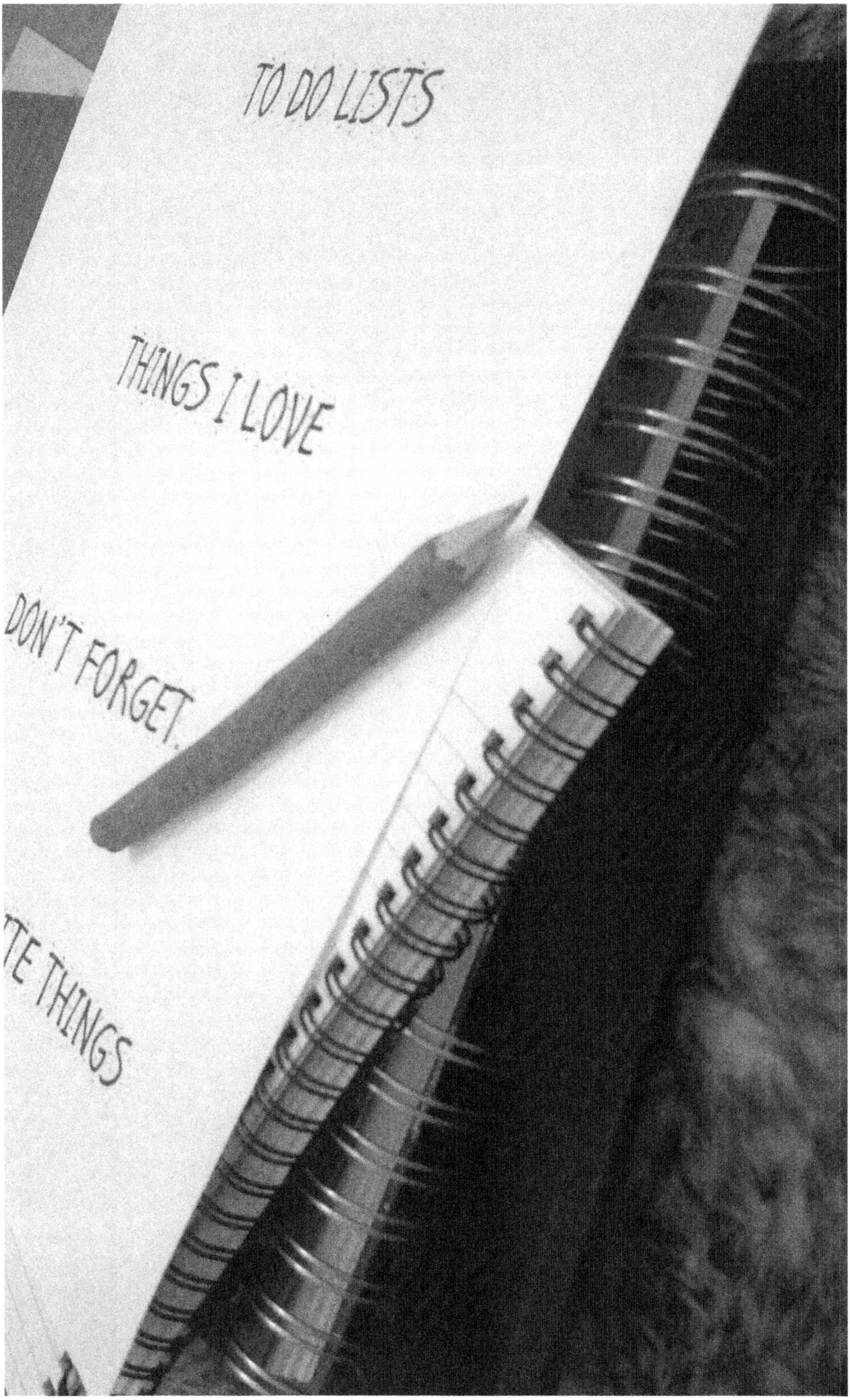
TO DO LISTS
THINGS I LOVE
DON'T FORGET.
TE THINGS

...For the LOVE of LISTS!

My list of 'SIMPLY NICE THINGS'...

✏️ ...For the LOVE of LISTS!

My list of THINGS that always BRIGHTENS things up!...

...For the LOVE of LISTS!

Count MY BLESSINGS...

✏️ ...For the LOVE of LISTS!

If I WROTE A SONG,
This is what I'd write...

...For the LOVE of LISTS!

What I have LOST RECENTLY...
& what I have GAINED...

✏️ ...For the LOVE of LISTS!

What I have FORGOTTEN that I LEARNED AT SCHOOL, That I would LIKE TO LEARN AGAIN...

✏️ ...For the LOVE of LISTS!

IF I wanted to WRITE A BOOK,
These are MY IDEAS...

✏️ ...For the LOVE of LISTS!

TASKS that give me JOY...

✏️ ...For the LOVE of LISTS!

**LIST of LINKS
to CALM my mind...**

✏️ ...For the LOVE of LISTS!

LIST of 'STUFF' that CALMS me...

✏️ ...For the LOVE of LISTS!

What I used to do, that I miss & would like to REDISCOVER...

✏️ ...For the LOVE of LISTS!

TODAY...From 1-10:
How STRESSED do I feel?
How fast is my MIND racing?
How HAPPY do I feel?

DATE: 'Emotion' 1-10:

Recognise when I need to make a change
or create a circuit breaker.

✏️ ...For the LOVE of LISTS!

Continued: TODAY...From 1-10:
How STRESSED do I feel?
How fast is my MIND racing?
How HAPPY do I feel?

DATE:　　　'Emotion'　　　　1-10:

Recognise when I need to make a change
or create a circuit breaker.

✏️ ...For the LOVE of LISTS!

<u>If I have the following symptoms:</u>
My head is drooped forward,
Tight shoulders,
Feel small,
No energy...
I MUST....

✏️ ...For the LOVE of LISTS!

My LIST of SEASONAL decorations...

SPRING: Blossom branches &....

SUMMER: Sand & pebbles from my favourite beach &...

AUTUMN: Conkers & leaves &...

WINTER: Twigs with baubles &...

✏️ ...For the LOVE of LISTS!

My LIST of SEASONAL ACTIVITIES:
'I spy' types of flowers,
Search sounds of nature,
Nature Mosaics,
Flower pressing,
Nature Collage,
Build a fairy garden &....

...For the LOVE of LISTS!

SOUNDS I shall LISTEN out for MORE to in each SEASON...

SPRING:

SUMMER:

AUTUMN:

WINTER:

✏️ ...For the LOVE of LISTS!

MY POEM about the SEASONS...

🖉 ...For the LOVE of LISTS!

CLUTTER... Things I really don't need:

✏️ ...For the LOVE of LISTS!

CLUTTER... 'Stuff' I should stop buying:

✏️ ...For the LOVE of LISTS!

MY TOOLKIT TO LIFE!
"To KNOW myself,
BELIEVE in myself,
Have CONFIDENCE
In myself"...

➡️

✏️ ...For the LOVE of LISTS!

MY QUALITIES...
What I find EASY &
What I am GOOD at...

✏️ ...For the LOVE of LISTS!

This is how I would DESCRIBE MYSELF...

✏️ ...For the LOVE of LISTS!

I am POSITIVE & STRONG
in these situations...

🖉 ...For the LOVE of LISTS!

This is how I DO or SHALL deal with FEAR...

✏️ ...For the LOVE of LISTS!

What I have done RECENTLY for SOMEONE ELSE,
That made me FEEL GOOD...

✏️ ...For the LOVE of LISTS!

What MATTERS to me...

✏️ ...For the LOVE of LISTS!

If I could do
SOMETHING DIFFERENT today,
what would I DO?...

✏️ ...For the LOVE of LISTS!

If SOMEONE LOOKED AT ME today what would they SEE?...

✏️ ...For the LOVE of LISTS!

I am UNIQUE now
BUT...
If I could be the 'perfect me',
I would LOOK LIKE?
I would FEEL?
I would CARE ABOUT?

✏️ ...For the LOVE of LISTS!

If I could
START MY LIFE AGAIN...
I would do this DIFFERENTLY...

✏️ ...For the LOVE of LISTS!

RIGHT NOW!...
What can I SEE?
What can I HEAR?
What can I SMELL?
How do I FEEL?

🖉 ...For the LOVE of LISTS!

LOOKING AHEAD...
'Something NEW!'
What would I like to LEARN?

✏️ ...For the LOVE of LISTS!

This is what I am going to do:
when I'm NOT trying...
...TO CONTROL EVERYTHING
...RUN EVERYTHING
...DO EVERYTHING
& THINK OF EVERYTHING...

"Letting GO & living LIFE!"

🖉 ...For the LOVE of LISTS!

What I would LOVE TO DO TODAY...

✏️ ...For the LOVE of LISTS!

My LIST...
Of what I DON'T want to do TODAY
& 'stuff' that
I DON'T WANT in MY LIFE?...

...For the LOVE of LISTS!

My LIST of 25 USEFUL USELESS 'Thoughts & Questions'...

1. Which celebrity would I swap places with?

2. If I could put one thing in a secret box, it would be:

3. The best food I've ever eaten is...

4. My favourite TV program when I was younger was:

5. If I was an animal, I would be..

6. My all time favourite song is: ...Or Top 3!

...For the LOVE of LISTS!

My LIST of USEFUL USELESS 'Thoughts & Questions'...

7. If I could automatically speak another language it would be...

8. If I could choose my birthday, the date I would choose would be:

9. If I could choose my full name, it would be:...

10. If I could live anywhere in the world, I would choose:

11. If I had to give away all my money, I would give it to...

12. My ideal house would look like:

✏️ ...For the LOVE of LISTS!

My LIST of USEFUL USELESS 'Thoughts & Questions'...

13. If I could choose any view from a window, it would be...

14. If I could have been the one to write a successful song, it would have been:

15. If I was the one who had invented it, my invention would be...

16. If I could have written any already successful book, I would choose:

17. If I could make up a new word it would be:
    ...which means:

18. My party trick is...

✏️ ...For the LOVE of LISTS!

My LIST of USEFUL USELESS 'Thoughts & Questions'...

19. If I was Queen for a day, I would...

20. If I could have any car or vehicle, I would choose:

21. If I could take a photo of anyone or anything, it would be...

22. If I could have 10 minutes with anyone, it would be:

23. If I could choose to have any skill, it would be...

24. My perfect career or job is:

25. If I could be professional in any sport, It would be...

THANK YOU...

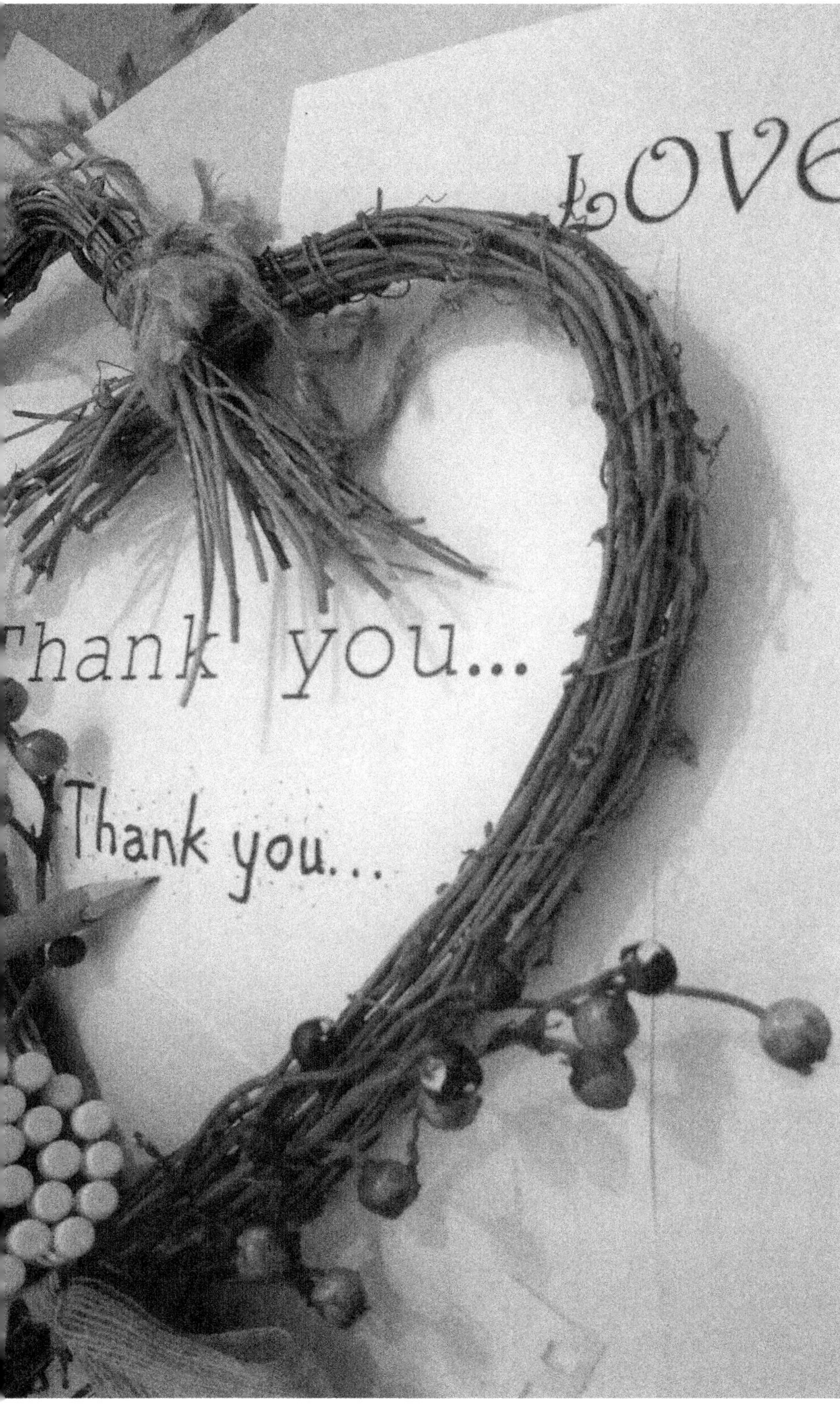
LOVE
Thank you...
Thank you...

✏️ ...THANK YOU...

..."A Smile &
A Thank you
Can go a long way..."

..."It has the power to
change someone's day
and MY own...☺"

...THANK YOU...

..."It's just **two little words** that can pack a punch when both said ...and NOT said!..."

...THANK YOU...

..."I must remember to praise & thank myself..."

Dear Self...

I wanted to say 'Thank you' because...

...THANK YOU...

My list of THANK YOU'S I want to send...

...THANK YOU...

TODAY I will THANK, & be Thankful for...

✎ ...THANK YOU...

If I could write a letter to ANYONE, I would write this to you BECAUSE...

MY FINAL THOUGHTS...

MY FINAL THOUGHTS...

"It's OK to rewrite MY LIFE"

Printed in Great Britain
by Amazon